Sell like a Champ

Mindsets, Toolsets, and Skillsets
for Peak Performance in Sales

Evan Sanchez

Mark,

You are a Champ!

Sell Like a Champ

ISBN-13: 978-0692920688
ISBN-10: 0692920684

To my beautiful wife Shelly and my precious children, Raegan, Jackson and Kennedy. May this book be a living reminder of my love for you and a guide for you to make a positive impact on the world.

DALLAS: The "Marcus Moore Employee of the Year" award for 2003 was presented to Evan Sanchez, Tarrant/Denton Bureau Sales Director. Evan's daughter Raegan was on hand to hear publisher Huntley Paton praise her father's single-handed salesmanship at the bureau office which resulted in a 16 percent sales jump for the year.

Evan Sanchez is the founder and CEO of Springboard Consulting. With the spirit of an entrepreneur, the mindset of a champion, the skills of a top sales performer and manager, the education of a psychologist, and the heart of a coach, he has worked with organizations and individuals for over twenty years to improve sales performance.

Contents

Acknowledgements

Thank you to all my teachers, coaches, my sister Maria, my brother James and especially my parents Janice and Larry for raising me with strong morals and teaching me what is important in life. Your love, insight, support and commitment provided me with the mindset I needed to find success in life.

Thank you to Richard VanCamp for being the best boss I have ever had the pleasure to work with and a special thanks for helping me with this book. Your work made this possible.

Thank you to Alison Cox for always being the bridge to our communications and helping me to find the right context and words to say. Your work made this possible.

Thank you to Shane Clevenger for being a great friend and helping with the design of the cover and your expertise, advice, and guidance.

Thank you to David Gideon for helping us bring it all together through our website, your expertise, and un-matched customer service.

Thank you to Sean Allen for helping me make the transition from sales manager to business consultant and Culture Engineer.

Introduction

Sell like a Champ is structured in a modular fashion. While you could certainly read it cover to cover, it's intended to provide bite-size chunks that can be read and applied for a sales team or for the person reading the book. You could say this book is to be used, not read and put on a shelf to collect dust.

This is not going to be your typical sales process, transactional tricks, tactics, or challenger versus consultative selling style development book. There are plenty of those already. The purpose of this book is to help you identify performance gaps that may be keeping you from higher levels of success in sales. This book will help you elevate your thinking, your actions, and your skills so you can grow the top line and increase take-home profits and commissions. The information is applicable to any business owner, entrepreneur, or sales professional regardless of industry, product complexity, current selling style, or performance level. If you are human and looking to make money in sales, this is for you. If you are an artificial intelligence bot or dislike humans, this is not for you.

Sell like a Champ is for you if you are an entrepreneur or an inventor with the next big idea. Believe it or not, you need to be the number one promoter (salesperson) and have high levels of energy, excitement, and passion for your business idea to come to fruition. If you cringe at the word "sales" or prefer titles such as "relationship manager" or "business development" because you "can't stand those pesky salespeople," then this book will empower you to positively change your own conscious or subconscious negative perceptions, self-talk, behaviors, or negative effects caused by opinions of others around you. We provide new ways of looking at sales so that you

1

can start to think like, act like, and sell like those performing at the top 10 percent in sales.

People already in the sales profession (my peeps) will benefit from being able to identify performance gaps in mindsets, toolsets, and skillsets in order to elevate performance. High-performing sales professionals will find ways to build resilience and stay strong in the sales profession. If you find it difficult to explain to others why you are successful, this book will help bring you clarity so you can help others. This knowledge will strengthen your confidence and improve your performance.

Studies show that the top 10 percent (those selling like a champ) would do well selling any product or service in any environment, and they work fewer hours than most of the salespeople in the bottom 20 percent (those selling like a chump). The top 10 percent have elevated levels of ambition and confidence while core to low performers have higher levels of anxiety and negative perceptions in most stressful situations. These individuals generally feel frustrated because they attend all the new trainings and apply social selling methods, but they may be struggling to pay bills with current sales commission earnings.

Organizations typically address sales performance gaps with more sales skills training, more product or service knowledge, and perhaps the latest customer relationship management (CRM) system. Once the basics are covered and a performer has shown some promise, higher-level expert sales training courses start to address key account management and advanced sales skill development. As a need for deeper knowledge and customer acquisition becomes more complex, strategic selling techniques are introduced into the skill-development mix. Most sales trainings focus on prospecting, asking questions, explaining features and benefits, handling objections, improving closing skills, managing time, and developing product or service knowledge. While these are important, they are not enough. If they were, we would not see such a wide gap in top performers (top 10 percent–sales champs, or "A" players), core performers (middle 70 percent–contenders or "B" and "C" players), and the (bottom 20 percent–sales chumps). This gap is caused by failure to address the building blocks to a winning mindset–creating the individual's ability to sustain high levels of confidence and ambition through positive beliefs, attitudes, and behaviors. In other words, product and service knowledge, sales skills, and the sales process must be supported by resilience and mental toughness, despite past failures and when facing the inevitable difficult circumstances that come with the sales profession. This is the key differentiator we address in *Sell like a Champ*.

A key distinction is that the top 10 percent have a "play to win" mentality. They believe they cannot fail. They believe that they can only learn and grow as they compete with themselves. They possess a positive belief that they are in a position to help others while sharing their message and living their passion versus the negative "I better do this or else" mindset. With this belief system in place, it is impossible for them to lose because in every struggle there is a lesson for future success that gives them strength to persevere.

These are the key guiding principles to keep in mind as you improve your performance thinking:

- Believe in yourself

- Believe in what you are selling

- Believe that selling is an honorable profession

- Believe in helping others

If you lack 100 percent confidence in any of these necessary guiding principles, you will not be able to be an "A" player and sell like a champ. You will always be a contender ("B" or "C" player) or even worse, a sales chump. Some of the ingredients to success are dependent upon you, and some are dependent on the company, product, or service you represent. Do you believe in what you are selling? If not, find a new company, product, or service to represent.

Here we grow!

Champions aren't made in gyms. Champions are made from something they have deep inside them—a desire, a dream, a vision. They have to have the skill and the will. But the will must be stronger than the skill.

—Muhammad Ali

Portrait of a Sales Champ

1. Sales champs look to build one another up and create a positive and engaged environment. This includes friends, family, clients, and coworkers.

2. Sales champs see challenges as opportunities to learn and grow.

3. Sales champs are not content living in comfort zones.

4. Sales champs have positive perceptions and exude confidence.

5. Sales champs are self-motivated, ambitious, and highly productive.

6. Sales champs provide value by solving problems, providing creative insights, and educating their customers.

7. Sales champs continue to learn and grow by challenging themselves, and others around them, to be the best they can be in their endeavors.

8. Sales champs are ethical and display character worthy of trust.

9. Sales champs possess strong relational and interpersonal skills.

10. Sales champs expect to win, and they meet or exceed quota.

If this sounds like you, this book will help you raise your awareness and provide actionable steps you can take to stay strong, build resilience, continue to sell like a champ, and produce results in any environment.

Portrait of a Sales Chump

1. Sales chumps experience lower levels of energy, and they are controlled by negative self-talk consisting of BMW (bitching, moaning, and whining).

2. Sales chumps suffer from LOF (lack of focus) and avoid challenges.

3. Sales chumps never have enough time, they experience constantly high stress levels, and they are generally disengaged.

4. Sales chumps suffer health issues on a regular basis.

5. Sales chumps are not open to learning and are controlled by fear and worry. Their mindsets are ego-based at best, and they are rarely satisfied.

6. Sales chumps look to place the blame anywhere but on themselves.

7. Sales chumps only win if they have the lowest price to pitch.

8. Sales chumps are always looking for the next sales tactic or trick.

9. Sales chumps are not making quotas and are not successful in growing their business. They are doing their best just to get by, day after day.

10. Sales chumps are afraid of the future and thus are in fear of losing; they play so as not to lose and not to meet their goals or quotas.

If four or more of the above sound like you, I dare you to read this book and take action. The time for change is *now*! Get engaged, and elevate your thinking. Your health and wealth depend on it.

Portrait of a Sales Contender

1. You are a core performer if you are neither a top 10 percent nor bottom 20 percent salesperson in your business category or team. You are considered a "B" or "C" player.

2. The portraits of both the sales champ and sales chump seem to describe you at various times in your sales journey. This could be because you are new to the sales profession or are perhaps a bit burned out or disengaged with your current situation.

3. You struggle with consistency in meeting your goals and quota.

4. There are times when it is hard for you to put in a full week's worth of work, and you are most likely working part time even if you have a full-time position.

If the above describes you, you are in an "adapting phase." This book and our programs are designed to help you elevate your mindset, and they provide the tools combined with skillsets to elevate you to sell like a champ.

Too often sales leaders focus on product, service knowledge, and sales skills alone. Or perhaps they use the latest technology app or customer relationship management tool to improve the performance of core performers. While these can be helpful, they will not help you to separate yourself from the pack and produce top 10 percent results in today's challenging sales environment. To do that, you will need to change your perceptions, your thinking, your behaviors, and your interpersonal and relational skills. You will need a new mindset and systematic rhythm for success. Doing so will increase the number of commas in your bank account and add joy to your life. You, too, can sell like a champ! Don't sell like a chump!

Think Like
A Champ

The battle to achieve sustained superior performance is often
fought in the mind.

Mindset #1

Belief

If you can see your vision for success and choose to believe, you will achieve.

If you believe you can, you will sell like a champ.

If you believe you can't, you will sell like a chump.

The Essential Need to Believe in Yourself

If you lack the self-confidence of a top 10 percent sales performer, it may be perceived instead as a lack of belief in your product or service. This will impact your ability to influence others, and your power to persuade others will dwindle. In turn, the lack of success negatively affects your belief in what you are selling, creating a cycle of negativity and doubt that makes it harder and harder to succeed.

When we underperform, we tend to look externally and blame situations or actions that are out of our control. Some of the most common complaints are poor lead quality, bad territory, lack of marketing support, insufficient product development, absence of sales enablement tools, and poor leadership/management practices. At times, some of these can be valid—perhaps your service or product is not meeting the current market needs, marketing is understaffed or under budgeted for growth, or you have a leadership team that is not aligned and not valuing the internal and external customer. However, most of the time, we are our own worst enemies. The championship mindset of the top 10 percent is what allows them to succeed, even when faced with these challenges.

Two things that a championship mindset will not fix are if you truly do not believe in your product or if you act in a dishonorable way. In this case, the honorable thing to do is to pass on selling this product or service because it will damage your personal brand and character, and you will never be able to sell like a champ for extended periods of time.

In order to sell like a champ, you must have a dream, a vision, and a desire to achieve something that is better that what exists today. You must be willing to do more than the average person. Your *vision* and *purpose* need to drive you each day. You have to be able to see them, believe them, and feel them in your mind and soul. Envision the future state as if it is real today and–even better–already happened. See yourself with your family on vacation, at a wedding, paying for your kids' school or college tuition, or driving the car you always dreamed you would have. These are all good examples that create an emotional attachment to future success.

While skill is essential, your will must be even greater than your skill to produce consistent championship level results in a fast-paced, technologically advanced, constantly changing environment.

 ## Performance Springboard

Success in sales is a choice. Make the choice to believe in yourself. Bring your best effort each day and build more confidence with each new customer. Don't let negative self-talk and self-defeat set in. Set attainable, action-oriented goals, such contacting a certain number of people each day or practicing your value proposition each day. Envision success and the feelings that go along with events that made you feel successful in your past.

Success is peace of mind attained only through self-satisfaction in knowing you made the effort to do the best of which you're capable.

–Coach John Wooden

Mindset #2

Build upon Strengths

Everybody is a genius. But if you judge a fish by its ability to climb a tree, it will live its whole life believing that it is stupid.

Albert Einstein

Build upon Your Strengths

Don Clifton, PhD, is known as the "father of strengths psychology" based on fifty years of studying excellence. This research founded two main discoveries that became the basis for the strengths-based methodology:

1. Successful people not only understand their talents and strengths but they build their lives upon them.

2. Successful companies don't just accommodate differences in employees but they capitalize on them.

Clifton identified thirty-four talent themes and has an assessment that can rank your thirty-four strengths from top to bottom. These strengths are the things you have the natural ability to do with consistent, near-perfect performance and will find joy and fulfillment doing. They are different from a talent. A talent is not a strength but a naturally recurring pattern of thought, feeling, or behavior that can be productively applied. I believe this distinction was made to show a difference in strengths-based assessments in comparison to behavioral or personality-based assessments. It is a different method due to its focus on the positive and exclusion of the negative. Most other behavior and personality-based tools equally look at strengths and weaknesses in their approaches.

Strengths can be underused or overused. Underused strengths are called "frozen strengths." They may become frozen for many reasons, but they are considered frozen when not used. This can be based on gender-specific expectations or family or societal pressures. For men, these may include empathy, connectedness, harmony, and positivity or WOO (winning others over). For women, frozen strengths sometimes include command, competition, self-assurance, and significance.

"Overused" is described as a talent used almost to the exclusion of all others. In my opinion, this is a direct link to low levels of emotional intelligence (EQ) when this occurs. Strengths combined with other behavioral, communication, and performance-based tools are all more powerful and provide a bigger picture for knowing ourselves and understanding how to improve our personal performance.

Utilizing your strengths is an exceptional strategy for development as long as you don't fall victim to a big fallacy I sometimes see in individuals and organizations: using the strengths psychology as a basis for allowing low EQ. Higher levels of emotional intelligence mean that you can be versatile. You don't make excuses for what you do, or do not do, based on your strengths or personality. You are responsible for your behavior. You must still be conscious of becoming the best you can be, and the better your EQ the higher your level of persuasion. Persuasion is key in sales and leadership. You have to convince others to trust you and believe in you to gain their business or allegiance. So know your strengths and apply them toward overcoming weaknesses while also improving your versatility and EQ.

 ## Performance Springboard

When addressing any weakness, we recommend building the skills, knowledge, and abilities necessary for growth by applying three to five of your top five strengths from the StrengthsFinder assessment. This technique will open the door for more success because you will be challenging yourself and building the higher-level thinking capability necessary to elevate performance. People working in their strengths are happier, less stressed, and extremely productive.

Do you know your strengths? If not, get strengths-based sales or leadership to get your assessment, so you know what behavioral strengths you have and can address areas needing improvement.

Mindset #3

Play-to-Win

Life is a game-are you playing not to lose, playing to cruise, or playing to win?

Play-to-Win Mindset

Gallup studies have revealed that only 29 percent of the workforce today is engaged at work. That is almost one-third of the total workforce, and that means that the rest are not performing at full potential. Sales champs play to win. If you are playing to win, you expect to be victorious and are willing to take risks versus playing it safe. This mindset accepts winning as typical and does not seem special to the sales champ because they have experienced winning before, and even when they lose, they find new ways to improve. They learn how to overcome the objection or situation that lost that deal, so they remain a champ! Sales champs maintain the play-to-win mindset and become more resilient over time.

If you are playing to cruise, you are "comfortable," and you avoid challenges and growth opportunities, such as training and development. You seek out sales positions with a steady base salary that allow you to pay the bills and take as many days off as possible. You are not selling like a champ and risk sinking further in your performance. Take a hard look at your life goals and passion for what you are selling. If you have passion for neither, you may need to find a new career. It may be that you are burned out or in need of an outside coach to help you refocus and get back on the path to being a contender and ultimately a selling like a champ.

If you are playing not to lose, you often experience mediocre to low performance. You expect to lose and play the blame game versus looking into the areas that you can improve. You do just enough to keep from getting fired. You are selling like a chump!

Winners identify their strengths and weaknesses so they can build a plan of attack, move forward, adapt, and overcome. Stick to your strengths, and utilize them heavily as you work toward your goals. Research has shown that strengths develop many times faster than weaknesses. Look for quick wins using your strengths to build momentum. Then apply those strengths to overcome an area that needs to be improved.

 ## Performance Springboard

Another way to build upon your strengths and overcome weaknesses is to proactively elicit feedback from your manager, coach, and/or peers. They can help you identify what you need to start doing, stop doing, and continue doing in order to take your performance to the next level. Always thank a person who provides constructive feedback. No matter how painful it may be to hear, they are doing you a favor and helping you grow.

Do you get excited and find new energy when it is time to perform, or do you find excuses to reschedule and avoid performing?

If you answered "yes," what can you do to put in more effort to build your skills or experience?

Mindset #4

Fear is Awesome

Fear is Awesome! Embrace your fear and seize the opportunity for growth. Awesome never comes from comfort zones. Fear is the gateway to awesome.

Sales Champs Find "Flow States"

As a sales professional, when have you experienced energized focus? Full engagement? Enjoyment?

These situations are links to times when you were highly focused, taking action for something worthwhile, and time seemed to fly by. You were most likely not worrying about what you were doing but instead living in the moment. These are high-performance experiences typically described as "being in the zone" by athletes. Identifying when you feel or have felt this way in the past can provide distinct insight on what is necessary to overcome mediocre performance. These experiences are called "flow states." In order to experience high-performance flow states more often, you have to balance the right level of challenge based on your current level of skill.

Practice is necessary to build confidence in your sales message, value proposition, transition, and closing skills for the product or service you are selling. If you do not believe in your product or you have not perfected your value presentation, your lack of confidence will show, and you will lose sales. You must believe in what you are selling and help others by solving problems and creating solutions to resolve client issues. You must practice until you exude confidence and competence.

Recognizing flow states enables you to unlock new levels of performance through the expansion of goals (bigger thinking/higher ambition), creativity (better problem solving), and the anticipation of future success (confidence).

More wins will begin to take place, positive energy will build, and you will experience what it means to think, act, and sell like a champ. Positive feelings of control and heightened energy, such as arousal (careful here—it's about energy), are precursors to finding your flow state. Feelings of relaxation can be a sign of not challenging yourself enough, and anxiety can be a sign of too much challenge given your current skill level. Both are adaptive, so they can be good and bad. This means you can use them to let you know you are on the right track or you are falling farther from flow depending on your current performance track. In other words, you are gaining momentum and seeing more success, or you're losing momentum and risk experiencing less success. In order to grow, one must continue to focus on skill development and challenge. Think of this as the throttle on a motorcycle. You must have the right balance in order to stay upright and be in the right zone for balance and speed. Feelings of apathy (lack of enthusiasm), worry, and boredom (lack of interest) are signs you may need to get some coaching to help you get back on track because you are not in a high-performance flow state. See flow psychology founder Mihaly Csikszentmihalyi's model below (Figure 1) to determine your emotional state of performance and the path to find flow for more success in sales.

 ## Performance Springboard

When was the last time you experienced a flow state? If you can recall a flow state, what beliefs, behaviors, attitudes, and language would you use to describe this time? Who in your circle of friends, peers, or mentors inspires you or is with you when these flow states occur?

If you have not felt the excitement of a "flow state" or "the zone" in sales, ask yourself, "Am I willing to put the work in and pay the price in extra effort to find success?" If not, stop "surviving," and look for the right job fit for your future success and happiness. If you have no other options, begin by building your presentation and value proposition skills while looking for more people to help.

High

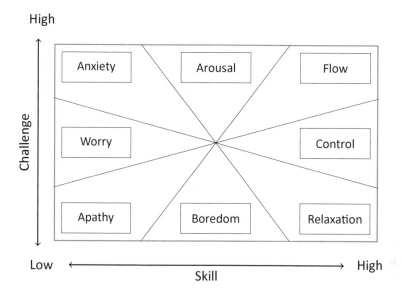

Figure 1: Emotional state of performance

What skills do you need to develop? What challenges have you been avoiding? What level of fear can you take on to find more success and be your best self?

What stands in the way, becomes the way.

–Marcus Aurelius, *Meditations*

Mindset #5

Power-of-Won

Champions visualize success and understand the Power-of-Won.

Power-of-Won Mindset

Success is accelerated when you envision the celebration after you have won, rather than winning itself. Motivation is about emotion. When you envision the reward of achieving your goal, that vision connects to your subconscious mind and creates the belief that it can happen. And in fact, the subconscious has no relation of time. Your mind creates belief that the vision has been achieved and therefore will happen again. Believe that if you can see and attach an emotion to the goal, it is already won!

Visualization is a tool that has been used for centuries. In the '90s, sports psychology started using visualization techniques and found that visualizing an entire match or performance had better effects on improving the outcome than only using physical skills practice. Visualization is not difficult to do and is very like daydreaming. To perfect this technique, all one has to do is add the intention and the desired outcome.

 Performance Springboard

- Sit comfortably upright, take three full breathes in, and exhale slowly.

- Focus on what the end results will look like and feel like.

- Develop crystal-clear, vision-leveraging strengths. Identify challenges, and set measurable goals.

- Connect internal vision and anticipation of future results. Seeing this as reality unleashes forces beyond you and engages higher-level consciousness to align opportunity.

- Base each level of necessary success in objective reality. You can't envision flying off a building without proper gear. Be real in your vision.

- This future state visualization creates high-performance creativity and a highly focused flow state that will elevate the levels of energy and drive needed to springboard you to the next level of success.

Mindset #6

Growth Mindset

The first and best victory is to conquer self; to be conquered by self
is of all things most shameful and vile.

—Plato

Growth Mindset

Mindset, the seminal book by Carol Dweck, a Stanford University psychologist, unpacks the difference between a fixed mindset and a growth mindset.

Growth (Champ Mindset)	Fixed (Chump Mindset)
Believes intelligence can be improved	Believes intelligence is static
Leads to a desire to learn	Leads to a desire to look smart
Embraces change	Avoids challenges
Persists in the face of setbacks	Gives up easily
Sees effort as a path to mastery	Sees effort as fruitless or worse
Learns from criticism	Ignores useful negative feedback
Finds lessons and inspiration in the success of others	Feels threatened by the success of others
As a result, reaches higher levels of achievement	As a result, may plateau early and achieve less than full potential
This gives them a greater sense of free will—true independence	This confirms a deterministic view of the world

Sales champs focus on growth. Sales champions do not enter the field and pick up the phone hoping to win. They enter the field and pick up the phone knowing they will face many *no's* on the way to a *yes*. The goal of each day is to practice, play, and improve. How you practice will determine how you play when the time comes to perform. Confidence and ambition are reinforced by practicing your craft with consistency and discipline. Putting the time in while being realistic about the timeframe necessary to accomplish a goal will keep you from feeling like you are failing to improve fast enough. In order to accelerate timeframes, one must leverage others around them, find mentors, build strong teams, and automate tasks whenever possible.

Sales champions manage growth by balancing drive and challenge. To reach the next level, there are always things you want to do and things you don't feel like doing. It is the degree of want, the desire, and the drive that determine whether you should or should not take the challenge necessary to grow. If you find yourself relating to the fixed mindset, these are key areas you should focus on in order to improve your performance.

Transformation from a fixed mindset to a growth mindset takes challenging your current ways of thinking and acting. The content below will help you to design a plan to adopt your growth mindset.

Focus

Sales champs possess intense discipline and mental focus. Focus is like a muscle that needs to be developed in order to accomplish difficult or long-term goals. Practice focusing on tasks that will bring you closer to your goal.

Focus requires stamina. Multitasking erodes the ability to focus. High-level focus must be developed. Schedule times on your calendar to focus on certain tasks during the day. You cannot pay attention to two activities, such as a lecture and a customer's needs. You will miss something because your focus is divided. Doing laundry while you work is multitasking that can be done effectively because the machine is doing the work while you focus on your task at hand.

Eliminate Distractions

Control the environment by reducing noise in your surroundings. Turn off notifications from your phone so that you can focus and accomplish your goals.

Exercise, Get Your Sleep/Rest, and Eat Every Three to Four Hours

Physical exercise helps to balance emotions and sleep patterns. Lack of sleep reduces your ability to think clearly and makes you impulsive and irritable. Not eating leads to depleted nutrients and be-ing "hangry"—hungry and angry—which leaves you unable to control your emotions and your focus.

Develop ways to physically symbolize throwing these thoughts away for good, such as picking up a blade of grass and throwing to the wind or writing chump behavior on a piece of paper, crumbling it up and throwing it away. This physical representation allows the mind to also visualize letting it go. Come up with positive affirmations that you can write down or put on your mirror in your bathroom or car to stay focused.

Develop Drive

Determine what you want to do, and do it. Take action immediately by making a plan and writing your goals on paper. Do not procras-tinate. Stick to the plan and mitigate distractions. Do not let feel-ings or old thinking patterns take you off track. Typically these early thinking changes should be short-term goals that will produce posi-tive feelings of success and accomplishment. These short-term wins build the confidence needed to persevere toward longer-term goals. These are the things you want to do.

Challenge Yourself

Determine what is you don't want to do, or what you perceive to be an obstacle. If relevant, make a plan to meet that challenge and transform it into a growth opportunity. What is the opposite think-ing you will need to adopt? What new behaviors can you substitute for the old behaviors? Find a support team that can help you stay focused on your behavior changes needed for success. Prepare by asking what you will do when you want to give up. Who can you call for support? What relationships can you leverage or activate? What resources will you need to guarantee your success? Preparing for potential problems and knowing what you will do in these times improves the probability you will reach your goal.

Practice Discipline

Self-discipline will be developed by putting in the time necessary to build the skills, knowledge, and behavior needed to reach the next level of performance. When practicing discipline, utilize focused and time-blocked activity. When will you do prospecting, prepare for sale calls, and conduct follow up activities?

You will also need to understand patience in setting timelines and expectations. Discipline is a very careful balance of focused time pursuing a goal and the patience needed to accomplish that goal. You will need to continually ask yourself if you are comfortable with the results and the timeframe necessary to do so. For example, when losing weight, it is recommended to lose one to three pounds of fat per week. If you lose more than this, it is a great feeling, and most people think this is what you want. However, there is also a greater risk that the weight will return if you go above what is optimal when it comes to weight loss. Disciplined and focused planning are essential for long-term change. Being patient, putting time in, and having the discipline to do this in the optimal way versus the fastest way will bring longer-lasting results when you are building new skills, knowledge, and behaviors. Real behavior changes can be seen immediately, but you can only say whether you have maintained that change if you have six months of success with your new behavior.

Build Competence

What level of competence do you have when exhibiting the new skills, knowledge, and behavior needed for growth?

Think about your level of performance on the competence ladder developed by Noel Burch:

1. Unconscious incompetence: You don't even know that you don't have the skills and knowledge to do what needs to be done to get the next level. This may have been your level of understanding for the growth mindset previous to this chapter. You will need to exercise more patience with yourself if you are starting from this level of understanding a new concept.

2. Conscious incompetence: You know there is a next level, and you know what you are missing. In this case, your goal should be to develop the necessary skills and knowledge needed for growth. The goal would be to become consciously competent and springboard to unconsciously competent to reach the peak performance levels.

3. Consciously competent: You know that you have the skills and knowledge necessary to perform. However, it may take a conscious effort to accomplish the task. You may need to check your work to be sure it is correct, or you may have to refresh your memory. At this level, more practice is needed to get to a level of mastery for the skills, knowledge, or behavior. Schedule time for practice to reach the next level.

4. Unconsciously competent: You perform the skill, knowledge, or behavior without effort. You are completely confident and can perform without thought, which leads to higher levels of performance and flow states. When teaching others, you will also experience higher levels of performance.

Performance Springboard

Which mindset do you find yourself relating to the most: growth or fixed?

What level of competence are you starting at? What does the next level look like for you?

If you relate more to the fixed mindset, begin transitioning to the growth mindset by talking to yourself in constructive ways, such as, "We will be successful! We can do this! I am great at this!" Champs believe in themselves and create ritualized self-talk to rewire *stinking thinking* that gets in the way of positive focus and breaks down confidence.

What are you telling yourself? If you are selling like a chump, it is hard to imagine and even seems silly, but this is the first step in becoming a champ. Ever hear of that children's book *The Little Engine That Could*? "I think I can! I think I can!"

If you think you can't, you will be right, and you will sell like a chump. Think you can, and you will be on your way to selling like a champ.

When you lose focus, how long does it take to regain and bounce back?

Look at rest patterns as well as eating patterns to make sure you are taking care of your physical body. Do you exercise enough? When you take care of your body, it allows you to stabilize emotions, focus the mind, and execute your purpose.

Mindset #7

Proactive Change

In business, change creates conflict; managing conflict effectively creates growth.

Proactive Change Mindset

Change starts in the mind, and it can be self-imposed, or it can come from outside force, such as getting cut from the team for unacceptable performance. The best way to handle change and growth is to accept what is needed to move forward and take action before change is forced upon you. Focus on the desired outcomes to create your vision for success. If you aim to be a high performer, it is important to accept your current performance reality! Your current level of performance must be measured and benchmarked against competition or best-demonstrated performances in your field.

Base the measures of successful change on facts and data when possible. Know your performance metrics:

- Where do you fall on the bell curve with your peers?

- What is your average deal size?

- How many deals do you need to close to make your quota or number?

- What is your win/loss ratio?

- How good are you at getting new appointments?

- How good are you at getting to root problems and real client needs?

- What leading indicators are you watching to measure success in the selling process and identify areas for skill development?

- How do these numbers compare to the top 10 percent?

If you don't know these metrics, find out! Numbers don't lie, and they point to areas for improvement or success markers to celebrate, hone in on the skills necessary, and master the results of true independence and proactive positive change.

Understanding and accepting your current performance gives you clarity for your future vision. Most of the average performers believe they are high performers because they feel like they are good at what they do. Having numbers to provide ranking and representation of reality is a good way to keep you from making yourself feel good about being average.

Simply put, you cannot continue to think the same, act the same, or be the same if you wish to improve. You will need to adopt an attitude of continuous improvement, curiosity, and the ability to picture yourself as a success. Don't play the blame game or make excuses. Be honest with yourself, and accept responsibility for the future. Visualize success, communicate, document your goals, act, and it will be yours—it will be done.

 ## Performance Springboard

Are you ready for change? What stage of change are you in when it comes to your sales performance reality?

1. I can't/won't change

2. Maybe I can change

3. Preparing to change

4. Taking action

5. Maintaining the change

6. Protecting the change

Describe what the next level feels like and looks like.

Ask yourself these questions:

- What beliefs, behaviors, attitudes, or self-talk will need to be altered to reach the next level of performance?

- What quantitative and qualitative measures can be used to track progress?

- Did I reach my goals for the day, the week, the month, or the year?

- What beliefs, behaviors, attitudes, and self-talk might be blocking me from reaching my full potential?

- What can I modify and focus on in the future that will bring the biggest payoff?

- What should the future look like and feel like?

- How will I celebrate?

Mindset #8

Expect Success

Each day is preparation for tomorrow's success.

Expect Success Mindset

Each day is preparation for tomorrow's success. Preparation to be the best you can be allows for magical things to happen, such as confidence, lower stress levels, and the ability to focus on achieving a successful outcome. The expectation and belief that you will be a success as you meet your challenges in life will make you unstoppable.

I learned the power of this mindset playing soccer. I had what was called an "educated foot." That meant that I could put the ball anywhere on the field of play with a high degree of accuracy. That made me a top pick for penalty kicks. As I prepared to take a penalty kick, I would walk up to the referees and tell them my number. They would give me a strange look and I would reply, "You need to know my number so you can record it in your book." I know this comes off as very arrogant, but the real truth is I was setting myself up for success. I envisioned success and expected it to happen.

The problem with the future is that the next steps are not always clear. You *must* develop strategies to take action and make your *vision* bend to reality. Expecting success helps strengthen confidence when what you expect is what happens.

Clarify Your Vision for Success

Your *vision* creates the will to develop the skills necessary to execute strategies and accomplish your sales professional growth goals. Sales is a lifestyle that empowers you when you are passionate and believe in your product or service. This translates into confidence and reduces self-defeat and self-consciousness. When buyers sense confidence, they will feel confident to buy from you because they can sense your belief in your solution, product, or service. As you close more sales, your passion will grow and become more visible to others as you execute your purpose. Your *vision* provides the motivation and emotional connection to drive success in the face of obstacles. Your *vision* guides your strategies, goals, and daily activities, and each day takes you one step closer to your dream. It feeds your will to work hard at becoming a "skillionaire" to become a millionaire.

 # Performance Springboard

Create a vision for ten years out. What does the next level of acceptable performance look like and feel like in your imagination? What about five years out? Three years out? One year? Six months? Three months? This month? This week? Today? Each day should bring you closer to your vision. This is a marathon that begins with one single step. That step begins today if you complete this exercise. Expect success!

Create a vision board that encompasses all your dreams for your life and your loved ones, coworkers, community, country, or world. No vision is too big for the vision board. You can draw, find clip art, or use magazines to build a vision board that you can see every day. Include pictures of what you want and who will be there with you. Expect this vision to become a reality.

Areas to consider:

- Physical health

- Emotional wellbeing

- Intellectual growth/personal development

- Spiritual fulfillment

- Social and cultural causes

- Occupational fulfillment

- Friends and family

- Fun

- Finances

- Anything you truly desire

Link Strategies, Goals, and Tasks to Execute Your Vision

In order to achieve your vision for success you will need three to five clear key objectives. At least two of these goals will need to be quantitative and based on sales performance and indicators of success. For example, sales quota achieved, commissions pay earnings, average deal size, or number of new customers.

Next create two to three qualitative objectives that you can focus on and be persistent in developing. These may include changes in beliefs, attitudes, behaviors, self-talk, knowledge, and/or skills necessary to achieve your vision of success.

Ask yourself, "What could go wrong?" If you are attacking a "big rock" weakness, how can you apply at least three of your top five strengths to overcome potential roadblocks? What will you do when something goes wrong? Take time to visualize yourself overcoming roadblocks. Practice what you will say and do.

Focusing on strengths creates more wins, provides more confidence among performers, and results in reasons to celebrate! Overcoming weakness will bring joy and new levels of success. Take time to celebrate with your team and your loved ones.

Mindset #9

Positive Mindset

We can't solve problems by using the same thinking we used when
we created them.
–Albert Einstein

Stinking Thinking vs. Positive Thinking

When negative perceptions take hold, there is a domino effect of negativity for you, others around you, and your company culture. Often, we forget that our perceptions are not necessarily reflective of reality. Perceptions create self-talk and our self-talk influences our behaviors, both positive and negative. If customers, prospects, or leaders perceive your actions or words as negative, their perceptions about you become negative and influence their behavior toward you, which only serves to confirm your negative perceptions about yourself if you suffer from "stinking thinking."

These negative perceptions about ourselves, what we call "stinking thinking," are the root cause of most underperforming sales representatives. This is where the championship mindset separates the top 10 percent of sales professionals from everyone else. Negative thinking and self-talk is what keeps average performers from reaching the top 10 percent. If you are confident that you have the product knowledge and the sales skills needed to get the job done, but you are still not getting the results you desire, it's time to take a hard look at your own stinking thinking.

Research by Dr. Martin Seligman in positive psychology has shown that we are born with a "set point" which can either be positive (optimistic) or negative (pessimistic). Knowing how we perceive things most of the time is important to be able to control our thoughts. This allows us to focus on our purpose and vision despite what our dominant inner voice may be telling us. Understanding our go-to behavior allows us to set intentional activity and take charge so we do not fall victim to our own stinking thinking. Current discoveries in neuroscience have gone further in showing that we can change our thinking and our thought patterns, even on a sub-conscious level. We no longer think that "we are who we are by age six," and that is our personality. That is a fixed-mindset belief, and science has proven this to be incorrect. You can transform yourself in a matter of weeks by rewiring any limiting beliefs and thinking patterns that may be holding you back by creating affirmations with what we should be saying to ourselves and repeating them three to five times a day. One thing is for sure—you will need to make the choice to change your thinking and commit to taking action!

We have all been told to be more positive at one time or another. This is much easier said than done, especially for those who have a set point that is pessimistic. It is an uphill battle but it is a battle that can be won. Consider the potential "flow states" that can be found if you have the "fear is awesome" mindset.

Sales Champs Reject "Stinking Thinking"

Chumps like to moan and complain. It takes lots of energy to complain. Use that energy for solutions and eliminate stinking thinking.

Sales Chumps Filter out the Good to Find the Bad

Chumps magnify the negative aspects of situations and relationships and filter out all the positive ones. For example, you had a wonderful day at work, completing your tasks ahead of time and being complimented for doing a speedy and thorough job. But that evening, you focus only on what you think you did wrong and forget about the compliments you received. Chumps have to retrain their minds to find the good instead of finding the bad.

Sales Chumps Take Things Personally

When something bad occurs, they automatically blame themselves or say they are sorry for something that they are not responsible for. For example, you don't hear back from a prospect after a sales meeting. Chumps assume that the deal is dead, or perhaps they no longer like you, or they didn't like your product or service. In reality, they may be having deep conversations about timelines and potential next steps. The champ would pick up the phone and give them a call to find out.

Sales Chumps Exaggerate

They automatically anticipate the worst and exaggerate situations for shock value. You spill something on your clothes, and you automatically think that the rest of your day will be a disaster. Champs can brush it off, change clothes, and make a new day focused on success.

Sales Chumps Cannot See Both Sides

They see things only as either good or bad. There is no middle ground or gray area. There is no ability to see the balance and strength in differences. Champs can turn on versatility and find a way to make the complex seem simple.

Selling Like a Champ Requires a Flip in Perspective

Most obstacles to selling success are in the internal messages and negative self-talk we send to ourselves. It is important to learn how to flip the perspective and tame the stinking thinking that can keep one from having success in sales.

Our prefrontal cortex is the only part of our mind focused on long-term goals. This voice sounds like this: "We need to prepare for that presentation." The dorsal striatum is another part of our mind that always wants to do what you did yesterday. This is the one that makes Mondays so difficult, and it sounds like this: "Has anyone liked my post on Facebook? Shouldn't I check e-mail again? Or should I just binge watch that new show I found Sunday on Netflix?" The nucleus accumbens is the pleasure party animal. This one says, "Work sucks–need more whiskey, wine, beer etc. to keep the party going. Let's forget about responsibility and goals."

Do you have your mind focused and aligned? Which area drives your behavior most? Setting long-term goals and aligning short-term milestones to measure success with a coach or manager helps to quiet the stinking thinking that can derail selling success. If you focus on the long-term goals and work on them daily, you get the prefrontal cortex and the dorsal working together to overcome influences of the nucleus accumbens. You will conquer yourself no matter your set point. Your intentions will come to fruition. Your mind will engage into creating the future and being successful in all that you do.

Chump Self Talk	Champ Self Talk
I've never been able to sell before.	It's an opportunity to grow and learn something new.
It's too complicated, and marketing stinks.	I'll tackle it from a different angle.
I don't have what I need.	Necessity is the mother of invention.
I am too busy to get this done	I couldn't fit it into my schedule today, but I can reexamine some priorities.
There is no way it will work.	I can try to make it work.
It's too radical a change.	Let's take a chance.
No one bothers to communicate with me.	I'll see if I can open the channels of communication.
I will never be good at this.	I will give it another try.

Change your thinking, so you can change your self-talk, so you can change your behavior, so you can sell like a champ!

Mindset #10

Intuitive Flow

When we combine intuition, action and challenging goals we elevate engagement and success in life.

Intuitive Flow Mindset

Sales Champs

- Believe in helping others

- Believe in themselves and are confident

- Believe in what they are selling

- Believe that selling is an honorable profession

- Have high personal integrity

- Know how to conduct a sales call

- Know how to advance sales situations

- Have elevated levels of ambition

- Utilize the right selling method at the right time

Sales champs believe in helping others, take action to solve problems, and create opportunities that bring value to their clients. They have the will to be the best at what they do and the desire to go the extra mile when it comes to servicing their accounts. Over time, this creates a reputation of success and goodwill that builds advocacy and influence with high-level decision makers. Many times, top performers know they are good but just don't know how to explain it to others, mostly because others would not understand or believe unless they had developed previously mentioned performance mindsets and mental capabilities. Sales champs are operating at the world-class and upper class consciousness levels. When combined, this level of thinking makes up the top 15 percent of the population.

Sales champs have access to the intuitive mind, and they can connect the rational mind in order to make dreams and visions become reality. This balance can be held for months at a time providing the ability to maintain high-level flow states. They have achieved what Abraham Maslow calls self-actualization, and through their work with their clients, they have reached transcendence. When a performer has reached unconscious competence, maintains a balance of challenging work, and applies high-level sales skills, their perceptions can remain positive during events that may cause others to drop in performance due to stress. The stress is used as fuel for action, whether that stress is good or bad. We call this peak performance mindset "intuitive flow."

The intuitive mind is a sacred gift, and the rational mind is a faithful servant. We have created a society that honors the servant and has forgotten the gift.

–Albert Einstein

Previous mindsets and findings highlighted in sports psychology, flow, and Abraham Maslow's hierarchy of needs provide the basis for unlocking the intuitive Flow mindset and creates the ability to consciously understand, create, and hold peak performance levels with this mindset. The challenges are overcoming stinking thinking, deficiency needs, negative self-talk, fixed beliefs, isolation, ungratefulness, and the selfishness of the ego.

Because there are key elements of belief necessary to achieve this level of peak performance, there is a need for "mindset stacking" to reach this peak performance state. Mindset stacking is the construction of new neural pathways by understanding the previous mindsets necessary to believe and achieve new levels of performance.

Combining the best mindsets to reach intuitive flow is similar to the need to have good nutrition and cardiovascular and anaerobic exercise to achieve peak physical condition. Applying these mindsets together works as a powerful combination to skyrocket success.

The strength in this mindset is the simplicity of its origin and the depth of the potential impact. It begins with an introduction to a single thought process aimed at creating positive self-talk and positive perceptions of self. Helping yourself and building positive perceptions allows you to help others more effectively. This creates a positive environment that builds positive experiences for friends, family, coworkers, and customers. Impact can expand to communities and policies to create a better version of what currently exists in alignment with one's *vision* for success. Key areas of focus to build and maintain this peak performance state include physical health, emotional wellbeing, intellectual strength and agility, spiritual connection and meaning, social awareness, and occupational engagement. Finding the right balance in these areas will elevate your thinking, your influence, your business, and your social impact.

Steps to Find Intuitive Flow

1. Accept your current reality. Develop a positive outlook and build a vision to become your best self. Move toward self-actualization.

2. Identify your deficiency needs using Abraham Maslow's hierarchy of needs, and plan to fill them. Deficiencies are anything listed below self-actualization. Focus on being your best self so that you can help others.

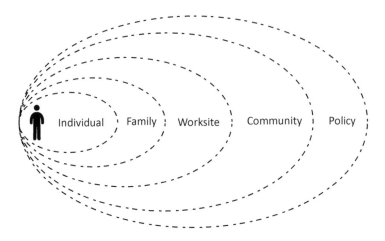

Figure 2: Finding the right balance

3. You must flip any fixed mind perceptions to a growth mindset. To do this, we recommend you focus on improving your health and your wealth in positive ways.

4. Be grateful for the levels you achieve. This accelerates your ascent to self-actualization, improves mindfulness, and allows you to link ideas for creative problem solving and relationship building. All of this creates improved performance in sales and business.

5. Look for challenges, and meet them head on. See them as opportunities for growth.

6. Conquer self. Take action to become the person you want to be the most by overcoming negative self-talk and limiting beliefs. Believe in yourself.

7. Once you have achieved self-actualization, develop or clarify a new personal vision, purpose, desire, or goal focused on helping others.

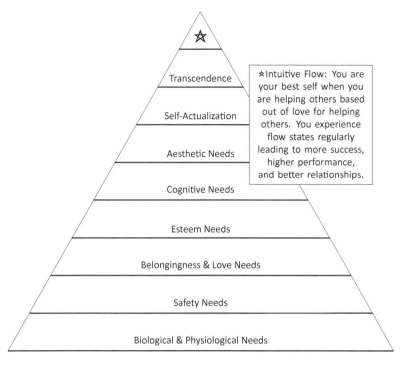

Figure 3: Emotional state of performance

8. Continue to develop intense mental focus capability.

9. Continue to develop mindfulness and practice awareness.

10. Know and apply strengths toward challenges, to find flow states.

11. Emotionally connect with your vision and be relentless in your pursuit of excellence. Be a champ in all that you do!

12. Connect with other high performers who will support your growth and help you elevate your own performance.

Performance Springboard

Embrace "accidental success!" If you associate with other high performer and do what they do, you will elevate your own performance.

Developing sales skills and the capability to recognize flow states enables you to unlock new levels of performance through the expansion of goals (thinking bigger/higher ambition) creativity (better problem solving), and the anticipation of future success (confidence).

What skills do you need to develop? What challenges have you been avoiding? What can you take on to find more success and be your best self? What can you do to add some fun and excitement in your life?

The most successful and powerful performers move from competing to creating, where the primary goal is to be the best they can be. Every day they are competing with themselves with the objective of being better than they were yesterday. They operate in an ego-free state of mind and see their job as a game. This way of thinking is rooted in a love and abundance spirit-based mindset. Dr. Abraham Maslow calls this level "self-actualization" or becoming all that one has the power to be. The most powerful performers operate at this level.

—Steve Siebold,
117 Mental Toughness Secrets of the World Class

Act Like
A Champ

Act Like a Champ

The "Act like a Champ" section will give you a score that reflects your current level of success based on a list of top ten behaviors that impact success in sales.

The key to creating positive change is to first have an idea of what success looks like and an understanding of the performance gaps that need to be improved. Taking action to close these gaps by changing behaviors, using new tools, building skills, and building knowledge will bring you success.

This section will show you what you need to do to act like a champ. Take the assessment, and look for areas to improve in the following sections.

We have provided behaviors, skills, knowledge, and tools to help you identify what you can do to improve for each behavior. Taking action to build new skills and behaviors will also improve your mindset as you change your behaviors and set intentions to improve and find success.

The final score will tell you if you are selling like a champ, a contender, or a chump.

Rate Your Champ Behaviors

❶   **❷**   **❸**   **❹**   **❺**

Never   Almost Never   Sometimes   Almost Always   Always

Know Yourself
You have a high level of self-awareness and possess the
ability to modify your behavior to build trusting relationships, reduce conflict, and maximize productivity.

Mentality of a Champion
You believe in yourself and possess high levels of confidence and ambition. You believe you cannot fail.

Energy Management
You have high positive energy and bring extra strength to
your team and environment, elevating the performance
of those around you.

Preparation for the Day
You prepare for the day the night before by linking short-
term and long-term strategies to accomplish goals.

Productive Time Management
You have a reputation of being on time and considerate
of others. You manage time effectively and efficiently.

Territory and Prospect Management
You have a strategic touchpoint strategy and technology
for managing existing and new business while managing
an acceptable cost of sale.

The Extra Mile
You work a forty-hour minimum workweek and identify
quarters or seasons to work harder than usual to reach
your next level of success.

Proactive

You have a proactive plan to deal with unexpected problems and opportunities.

Professional Internally and Externally

You treat prospects, customers, and your internal teammates with the same level of respect and professionalism.

Commitment and Perseverance

You stay strong and focused, and you have the ability to be committed long term while enduring stress, discomfort, and temptation.

Total:

What does your total score mean?

If you are selling like a champ, your score will fall in the range of forty-five to fifty.

Nice work! What can you do to stay strong and build resilience? Review your behaviors, and envision the next level. What mindsets could elevate your thinking and elevate those around you?

If you are adapting—either becoming a champ or falling toward chump land—your score will fall in the range of thirty-eight to forty-four.

What mindsets can you apply to areas where you scored the lowest? Make these your priorities for growth. Leverage your strengths to build a plan of action. Envision where would you like to be in the next three months.

If you are below a thirty-eight, you are selling like a chump

It's a good thing you have this book. Accept where you are, and let's focus on your vision and purpose to find the emotional drivers to motivate you. Doing this will get you out of chump land. We'll next focus on your strengths and build a plan of action. We may want to start with a 10Rule mindset assessment to accelerate results.

Ask yourself these questions:

- What can I do to improve?

- Why did I give myself that score?

- What am I doing right?

The following pages will dive deeper into each behavior, so that you can gain the knowledge and toolsets necessary to achieve your vision of success and create actionable steps to sell like a champ.

Know Yourself

Know Yourself and Others

People like to buy from other people that they know, like, and trust. There are certainly instances where someone has a product or service that cannot be purchased elsewhere, but not for long. If they find the product or service somewhere else with someone they know, like, and trust more than you, the buyers will leave the first chance they get.

So not only is it important to know yourself and your behaviors—the things you say and do, the things that motivate you, your likes and dislikes, and your preferred pace and topics of conversation—but it is also important to control yourself if you see that your actions are creating negative tension and frustrations for the buyer or customer. More importantly, realize your prospects' and customers' preferred behavioral styles (know others) so that you can modify your actions to make them feel comfortable and reduce potential interpersonal tensions and objections that may get in the way of making a sale.

Developing higher levels of self-knowledge and self-control is necessary for relating to others and closing more sales faster. This displays higher levels of emotional intelligence and interpersonal and relational skills.

Current tools that help you understand your preferred behavior and personality include Myers-Briggs, DISC, Social Styles, Predictive Index (based on social styles), StrengthsFinder, leadership 360s, and the next level 10Rule performance-thinking algorithms and their subconscious drivers of behavior. These are helpful in gaining a better understanding of yourself and how you can better serve others.

Knows self and others–the power of emotional intelligence. Having the ability to recognize and understand emotions in yourself and others, and the ability to use this awareness to manage your behavior and relationships.

–Emotional Intelligence 2.0

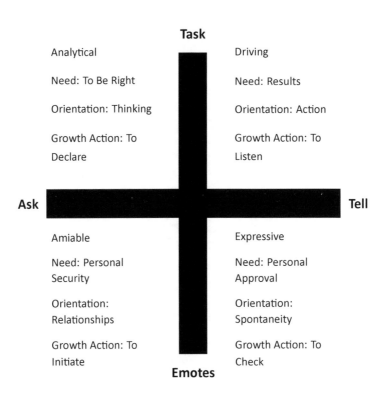

Figure 4: Tracom social style model

The social style model helps us know our preferred style based upon assertiveness (asking or telling), responsiveness (emotion), and relationship-driven versus task-driven controlling emotions (controls).

Using this toolset and skillset can help you in several ways:

1. Know yourself.

2. Identify personal growth actions.

3. Identify others' preferences for improved communication, engagement, and productivity.

The social style model helps us to know our preferred behavior and communication style based upon behavioral preferences regarding assertiveness (asking or telling) and responsiveness (emotion or task).

Emotional intelligence accounts for about 58 percent of performance in most jobs. Because of our brain's wiring, it is a biological fact that our first reaction to any event will be an emotional one, but only 36 percent of people are able to accurately identify their own emotions as they happen.

Get Anyone to Buy from You

Know yourself. The first level of emotional intelligence is the ability to know yourself, your preferences, and the impressions you make on others. This includes your strengths, weaknesses, and impact on others around you.

Control Yourself. The second level of emotional intelligence is the ability to control yourself. To build trust, be tolerant of other preferences.

Know Others. In the third level–observing other behaviors–you understand others' communications needs, preferences, and methods of dealing with stress.

Do for Others. In the fourth level, you know what others want and prefer. You actively and knowingly modify your behavior to build trust, making is easy for others to buy from you.

EMOTIONAL INTELLIGENCE	VERSATILITY
Self-Awareness	Knows Self
Self-Management	Controls Self
Social Awareness	Knows Others
Relationship Management	Does Something for Others

Versatility: having the ability to adapt one's behavior to meet the challenges and associated stresses, including the following:

– Business model disruption

- Heightened customer expectations

- Diverse customer and employee demographics

- Agile business processes

- Rapidly changing technology

- The social media explosion

- Demanding performance expectations

- Cutthroat competition

- Evolving societal mores

- Changing government regulation

By 2030, over 2 billion jobs will disappear. Will your job be one of them? What are you doing to prepare for this uncertainty? I think that versatility is the key competency of the future.

–Thomas Frey

Knowing Your Strengths and Your Social Style is a Powerful Combination

Tracom Corp, the developers of Social Style training, published a whitepaper showing how the thirty-four strengths correlate with the social style model. Knowing your top five strengths can also provide insight into your natural ability (talent) for high versatility. If you have one strength from each social style quadrant in your top five strengths profile, you most likely have an elevated level of versatility. You can leverage your ability to gain trust from many types of buyers for big-time payoff in sales.

If your strengths all fall into one social style quadrant, you are mostly likely going to have to work on your versatility if you are going to be able to sell to a large prospect base and increase your close ratio. You want to be able to build trust with at least 60 to 75 percent of people. The 25 percent who are like you is the easy part. Adding another 50 percent (two other styles that trust you) improves your close ratios.

Remember, versatility helps to build relationships based on trust, and people like to buy from sales champs who provide value and are likeable and trustworthy.

The thirty-four strength themes are organized within these four leadership dimensions, as shown in the following table. This table also shows the relationship of the leadership dimensions and themes in relation to the social style model.

EXECUTING	INFLUENCING	RELATIONSHIP BUILDING	STRATEGIC THINKING
Achiever	Activator	Adaptability	Analytical
Arranger	Command	Developer	Content
Belief	Communication	Connectedness	Futuristic
Consistency	Competition	Empathy	Ideation
Deliberative	Maximizer	Harmony	Input
Discipline	Self-Assurance	Include	Intellection
Focus	Significance	Individualization	Learner
Responsibility	WOO	Positivity	
Restorative		Relator	
DRIVER	EXPRESSIVE	AMIABLE	ANALYTICAL

Performance Springboard

DRIVER

Wants to Know	Tunes in if You Are	Responds if You
What are the opportunities?	Competitive	Focus on the bottom line
What's the bottom line?	Enterprising	Responsive
Who's in charge?	Idealistic	Initiate action
What's next?	Fast moving	Show competence

EXPRESSIVE

Wants to Know	Tunes in if You Are	Responds if You
Is it fair?	Respectful	Demonstrate worth
Can I help?	Assuring	Show loyalty
Is it best?	Accepting	Think of others
Will it benefit all?	Idealistic	Are a team player

AMIABLE

Wants to Know	Tunes in if You Are	Responds if You
What are people's opinions?	Social	Are tactful
Is it disruptive?	Flexible	Use a light touch
Can it be changed?	Informal	Show how you fit in
Will it gain acceptance?	Accepting	Get along

ANALYTICAL		
Wants to Know	**Tunes in if You Are**	**Responds if You**
How does it work?	Unemotional	Do your homework
Who does what?	Inquiring	Are precise
Can we sample?	Factual	Use logic
What are the tradeoffs?	Practical	Progress slowly

- How self-aware are you? What thoughts, emotions, and actions help/hinder you achieving exemplary sales results?

- How effective are you at modifying your social style to mirror the styles of your buyers?

- What actions are you taking to increase your versatility?

- Given different social styles, how confident are you that you can close business with 60 to 70 percent of the people you meet?

Mentality of a

Champion

Characteristics of Mentally Tough People (Amy Morin, *Huffington Post*)

- Practice gratitude.

- Accept challenges as opportunities for growth.

- Focus on things they can control.

- Set healthy boundaries.

- Take calculated risks.

- Make peace with the past.

- Learn from their mistakes.

- Create their own definition of success.

- Set aside time to be alone—develop mindfulness.

- Accept responsibility for their lives.

- Practice perseverance.

- Modify unhealthy beliefs.

- Expend mental energy wisely.

- Practice realistic optimism balanced with critical thinking.

- Tolerate discomfort.

- Stay true to their values.

Five Levels to Mental Toughness (Larry Wilson and Steve Siebold)

1. Playing Not to Lose: "I'd better perform, or I'll be in trouble." Those performing at this level are doing just enough to avoid getting fired. This fear-based approach describes the reactive, defensive mindset of an order taker.

2. Playing to Cruise: "As long as I continue to perform, I can cruise."

   These performers are mentally cruising through the job without really engaging in any serious thought. In other words, they are doing just enough to get by.

3. Playing to Improve: "Maybe I can accomplish more than I thought. Maybe I'm better than I think I am."

   At this level, performers begin to actively engage their thoughts and feelings in the task at hand, attempting to get better. It is the beginning of an upward ascent for the performers, which is usually triggered by a belief-altering event that makes the performers believe they may be capable of more.

4. Playing to Compete: "I think I can be the best!" Performers begin to believe they are capable of beating out their competition and being the best. This level is primarily ego-based, where winning is the main objective. The ultracompetitive ego-based performers are proving they are the best, which is rooted in a fear and scarcity mindset.

5. Playing to Win: "I cannot fail; I can only learn and grow. The only person I'm competing with is myself. I no longer feel fear

because it's impossible for me to lose. I feel so grateful just to have an opportunity to be the best I can be. I see my performance as the primary catalyst of my self-actualization. I don't have to be who I've always been. I learn, and I grow–that's how I win."

 ## Performance Springboard

Note that levels one through four are fear and scarcity mindsets. Only level five is a level of true independence as outlined in 10Rule, and it is based in the positive love and abundance mindset. Where are you?

What mindset(s) do you need to apply to reach the highest level?

Develop Mental Toughness (Steve Siebold)

Becoming mentally tough is *tough*. Get a coach!

Most middle-class thinkers (as opposed to world-class thinkers) are mildly to extremely delusional regarding their career skills, work ethic, attitude, goals, etc. This delusion interferes with attaining higher-level performance.

A salesperson who believes she is world-class will continue to make excuses and blame others as she continues to manifest middle-class results. She will remain confounded and excuse-prone until a world-class coach steps in and coaches her into objective reality.

- What characteristics of mentally tough people do you exhibit? What characteristics would you like to develop?

- What stinking thinking patterns are holding you back from achieving success? How will you overcome those patterns?

- Commit to being the best, and play to win. Believe that you cannot lose but only learn and grow.

- Be positive: reframe negative thoughts to flip the perspective and eliminate stinking thinking.

- Rehearse situations: imagine dealing with real events and how you will overcome adversity.

- Manage energy: practice breathing exercises and relaxation techniques to calm you during intense situations.

- Set goals: develop a sense of purpose, and plan time to achieve it.

- Control focus: develop mindfulness in all situations, regardless of the level of stress.

Energy

Management

Energy Management

Jim Loehr and Tony Schwartz are two sport psychologists who wrote a bestselling book called *The Power of Full Engagement*. They found that managing energy, not time, is the key to high performance and personal renewal. Their studies align with and provide science-based validation of our own peak-performance coaching program, Intuitive Flow.

Finding intuitive flow starts with managing perception and finding ways to transfer protective energy into productive energy. Perception is very powerful—when we have positive perceptions, positive attitudes will follow. Focus is improved and distractions are minimized, so we can get more done in less time. Having more energy provides more time and efficiency to get things done while activating intrinsic motivators such as achievement, recognition, and growth. Work and life become fun when you accomplish goals and celebrate success. More positive emotions are experienced on a daily basis, and self-esteem improves, elevating belief in yourself. This helps to eliminate stinking thinking and creates a springboard for an upward spiral of positive energy.

Attitude matters in sales. Who wants to meet with the sad, angry or depressed sales person?
Choose positivity and joyfulness. Start with the body to improve emotional stability.

The mood list below is from The Power of Full Engagement. What moods do you experience more often: protective (negative) or productive (positive)?

(CONTENDER)	(CHAMP)
High Negative/Protective Energy	High Positive/Productive Energy
Angry	Invigorated
Fearful	Confident
Anxious	Challenged
Defensive	Joyful
Resentful	Connected

(CHUMP)	(CONTENDER)
Low Negative	Low Positive
Depressed	Relaxed
Exhausted	Mellow
Burned Out	Peaceful
Hopeless	Tranquil
Defeated	Serene

If you are on the negative side, change needs to start with your perception and self-talk. Focusing on the body will provide the foundation for positive self-esteem and belief in yourself. Focusing on the body builds productive energy and opens the gateway for highly positive and productive activity that will lead to success in sales.

Positive moods to increase your ability to sell. No one wants to spend time with someone who is sad, tired, angry, or depressed. No one wants to listen to bitching, moaning, and whining, either. If this sounds like you, not only will you have issues managing your time and close fewer sales but you will also have a less fulfilling life. Your happiness and success is up to you—no one else. Accept this reality, and take care of yourself.

Manage stress by developing positive rituals. Regular exercise, eating, and sleeping habits reduce stress and create the ability to sell in any environment. Make sure you are actively working your muscles and cardiovascular system and eating nutritiously for energy and fuel. It is difficult to focus on the task at hand if you have not eaten or are falling asleep, or even worse, you're so sick and emotionally spent you can't work. Taking care of your health is key to stabilizing your moods, improving focus, and creating positive energy. Positive energy makes you more positive, and it makes others more attracted to you. In sales, you want to bring positive energy and not suck it away and bring negativity. Champs bring energy, and chumps suck. Once you understand how to manage stress, you can make a positive impact on others around you. This will also help you to become more resilient. This resilience can then expand and grow to improve your environment.

Stress is the global health epidemic of the twenty-first century.

–The World Health Organization

Leading Causes of Workplace Stress

- 46 percent: workload

- 28 percent: people issues

- 20 percent: juggling work/personal Issues

- 6 percent: lack of job security

Cost of Stress in the Workplace (Jacquelyn Smith, Business Insider, 2016)

- One million workers a day miss work, costing companies $602 per employee per year. Health-care costs for stressed employees are 46 percent higher than for nonstressed employees.

- Absenteeism: Employees not functioning at 100 percent due to stress cost companies $150 billion per year. Absenteeism is to blame for 26 percent of health-related production loss.

- Employers spend $300 billion per year for health care and workdays missed because of stress.

The Keys to Managing Stress—a Mindset (Tracom Model)

How you filter information and interpret the world:

- Personal beliefs

- Realistic optimism

- Personal responsibility

How you act when challenges arise:

- Self-assurance

- Self-composure

- Problem-solving

- Goal orientation

How you interact and communicate with others:

– Courageous conversations

– Social support

Energy Management (Rich Fernandez, *HBR*, June 2015)

How to develop resilience:

– Exercise mindfulness: visualize the end state; pause without emotion or judgment; connect the thoughts, behaviors, and emotions needed to attain the vision.

– Compartmentalize the cognitive load: we receive 11 million bits of information every second, but we can only process about forty bits.

– Take detachment breaks: mental focus, clarity, and energy cycles are typically ninety minutes to two hours.

– Develop mental agility: pause, step back, reflect, shift perspective, create options, and choose wisely.

– Cultivate compassion: be sympathetic to, and address the difficulties experienced by, yourself and others.

– Maintain a healthy lifestyle: make exercise and nutrition a priority.

– Practice positivity: positive emotions include joy, gratitude, serenity, interest, hope, pride, amusement, inspiration, awe, and love.

The Power of Positivity (Barbara Fredrickson, Wellcoaches)

People who cultivate positivity have several important traits:

– Open-minded

- Flexible

- Mindful

- Optimistic

- Social

- Healthy

The tipping point ratio needed for positivity is three to one–three positive emotions to every negative emotion. Data shows that 80 percent of people are languishing below the three-to-one tipping point.

Energy Management: Build Positivity through Coaching

Coaches help you achieve a variety of things:

- Build positive emotions

- Connect health and well-being to a higher purpose in life

- Create a vision for the future with a doable action plan

- Uncover strengths and talents leading to goal attainment

- Set stretch goals that are engaging but not anxiety producing

- Foster trust, rapport, and connections with others

- Identify inspiring role models, mentors, and heroes

- Laugh at self and situations

- Improve awareness and enjoyment associated with thriving

- Appreciate life's gifts, including challenges

- Stop to savor moments of contentment

Initiatives and programs fostering resilience in the workplace returned $2.30 for every dollar spent in the form of lower health care costs, higher productivity, lower absenteeism, and decreased turnover.

 ## Performance Springboard

What personal and/or professional situations are creating negative stress in your life?

What actions are you taking to address the stress associated with these situations?

What actions will you take to develop your resilience in the face of a world with constantly increasing demands, complexity, and change?

Initiatives and programs fostering resilience in the workplace returned $2.30 for every dollar spent in the form of lower health care costs, higher productivity, lower absenteeism, and decreased turnover.

Are you interested in a shortcut to identify what is keeping you from selling like a champ? Go to www.SellLikeAChamp.com today to find a special opportunity to get your assessment today.

Discoveries in neuroscience are making performance-thinking drivers visible and providing the data necessary to identify the specific thinking patterns that directly impact high performance and low performance. These groundbreaking tools allow organizations and individuals to assess high performance thinking patterns with a fifteen-minute assessment. This is not a normal behavioral assessment. This is performance-based analytics that can transform root-cause stinking thinking in a matter of weeks, similar to flipping your self-talk from chump to champ!

For organizations it opens the door for huge savings and improved hiring, benchmarking, development, and advanced auditing for quantitative performance analysis.

These Performance Thinking Algorithms (PTAs) were discovered Gary Morias and patented in 2014 as part of his 10Rule platform. This is a real breakthrough in performance and wellbeing. The cloud platform and its science-based metrics provide a new preventative behavioral healthcare solution that also improves productivity. The key to this strategy is to sustainably replicate the top 10 percent performers for each role in the organization.

The key to high performance rests on that individual's performance thinking. Performance thinking links directly to the intangible qualities we often struggle to describe: the "It" factor, will, heart, drive, versatility, agility, and more. In short, these are qualities of people who have real independence, drive, and capability to achieve. They are selling like champs!

One of the major challenges for organizations is creating a common performance language for the culture and driving employee engagement around the performance improvement process while also linking those to capabilities, developmental paths, and measurable results. Due to the soft-skill nature of many of these capabilities, it is very difficult to show ROI and quantitative data. You may know success when you see it, but that doesn't mean you can replicate it.

By identifying and defining the underlying characteristics that make individuals successful in a specific role within a specific organization, individual performance can be framed in terms of developing adaptability, versatility, ability to manage stress, and drive. Rather than repeatedly sending a group through skills training, everyone receives feedback and clinically validated coaching to develop and improve underlying thinking patterns that are driving unwanted behaviors (false independence) and holding them back from success. Individuals and organizations can now develop thinking patterns that lead to real independence, ambition, confidence, and success.

Creating a culture based on top-performance thinking creates alignment and builds resilience against underperformers pulling down high performers. All organizational cultures suffer from this deviation to the mean, but with 10Rule that no longer has to be accepted.

Sales champs mitigate stinking thinking (fear and stress motivators) and develop performance-thinking algorithms associated with real independence and self-motivation.

Sales champs are self-motivated and possess high ambition, confidence, relational, interpersonal, and systematic thinking capability.

Sales chumps maintain fear and scarcity mindsets that create stress and anxiety. This increases unease. This leads to disease in the body and mind connection with direct impact on employee engagement, presence, healthcare costs, and all areas of wellbeing, including your health and your wealth.

Preparation for the Day

Preparation for the Day

High-performance salespeople spend their time meeting customer expectations, conducting research and analysis, and developing their capability. What percentage of your time is currently spent in these areas?

If your answer is less than 50 percent, what activities will you change to make more efficient and effective use of your time?

- Customers believe that sales reps are 88 percent knowledge-able on product and only 24 percent knowledgeable on customer business issues (Corporate Visions).

- Seventy percent of people make purchasing decisions to solve problems. Thirty percent make decisions to gain something (Impact Communications).

- The top sales people use LinkedIn at least six hours per week (the Sales Management Association).

- Fifty-seven percent of B2B prospects and customers feel that their sales teams are not prepared for the first meeting (IDC).

Champions do not become champions when they win the event, but in the hours, weeks, months, and years they spend preparing for it. The victorious performance itself is merely the demonstration of their championship character.

—T. Alan Armstrong

World-class sales champs prepare in these ways:

- Monitoring industry and market trends

- Staying abreast of customer issues

  - Strategic performance

  - Operational threats and opportunities

- Understanding customer buying processes

- Developing thought leadership positions

- Conceptualizing innovative, holistic solutions to customer problems

- Generating weekly sales plans and daily call plans with metrics

- Reviewing customer notes pertaining to previous interactions

- Visiting LinkedIn to ascertain business connections

- Checking social media posts to identify hot-button issues and client interests

- Developing comprehensive precall plans

- Practicing client calls and presentations

- Analyzing competitor intelligence

- Developing sales skills—transactional, challenger, and consultative based on your industry, product, service, and buyer

High-performance salespeople *should* spend their time in these activities:

- Meeting customer expectations

  - Developing social media content

  - Contacting prospects via social media

- Precall planning and practice

- Meeting preparation

- Interviewing prospects to understand their problem(s)

- Providing solutions and thought leadership

- Conducting research and analysis

  - Industry trend research and analysis

  - Client-specific issue identification and analysis

  - Prospect and territory research and analysis

  - Using CRM to update client records and analyze trends

- Developing capability

  - Weekly meetings with managers to review performance and receive coaching

  - Ongoing capability development

 ## Performance Springboard

Proper planning and preparation are more than simply part of your selling process—they are a way of showing interest and respect to your potential or existing customer. Coming into a meeting with a solid foundational understanding and well-planned strategy will prove your professionalism while helping to build professional trust.

—Nick Kane

How do you keep abreast of industry, market, and client issues?

How have you demonstrated thought leadership during the past twelve months?

What technology and social media platforms do you use in support of servicing your clients? How do you prepare for each client interaction?

Productive Time Management

Time Management Guidelines for Success in Sales

1. Sixty percent of your time should be client-focused–for example, sales meetings, lead qualification, sales meeting prep, and follow-up work.

2. You should hold three to five objective-based sales meetings weekly, focused on moving closer to a new customer or sale.

3. Spend a minimum of six hours a week, prospecting/networking.

4. Get rid of clients who buy only on low price and want lots of attention.

5. Know your clients, and treat them with the necessary amount of attention based on their relationship and loyalty to you, as well as the size of the account

6. Make sure your top-ten clients get you whenever they need you.

7. Don't neglect or forget about clients who are in your top ten but are not needy. Find ways to provide value, or your competition will.

Lack of direction, not lack of time, is the problem. We all have twenty-four hour days.

–Zig Ziglar

Self-Assessment: Time Management

In the table below, check the ten highest "How I *actually* spend my time" sales activities. Next, check the ten highest "How I *would like* to spend my time" sales activities.

PLANNING	HOW I ACTUALLY SPEND MY TIME	HOW I WOULD LIKE TO SPEND MY TIME
Industry Trend Analysis	☐	☐
Client Business Analysis	☐	☐
Annual/Monthly Sales Plan	☐	☐
Weekly Activity Plan	☐	☐
Precall Planning/Practice	☐	☐

PROSPECTING	HOW I ACTUALLY SPEND MY TIME	HOW I WOULD LIKE TO SPEND MY TIME
Social Media Selling	☐	☐
Prospect Research	☐	☐
Contacting Prospects	☐	☐
Asking For Referrals	☐	☐
Developing Sales Collateral	☐	☐
Speaking at Conferences	☐	☐
Attending Marketing Events	☐	☐

SELLING	HOW I ACTUALLY SPEND MY TIME	HOW I WOULD LIKE TO SPEND MY TIME
Qualifying Leads	☐	☐
Meeting Preparation	☐	☐
Approaching Prospects	☐	☐
Interviewing Prospects	☐	☐
Providing Thought Leadership	☐	☐
Developing Proposals	☐	☐
Negotiating Terms	☐	☐
Closing Business	☐	☐

ADMIN/OTHER	HOW I ACTUALLY SPEND MY TIME	HOW I WOULD LIKE TO SPEND MY TIME
CRM Data Entry	☐	☐
Preparing Internal Reports	☐	☐
Attending Noncustomer Meetings	☐	☐
Developing Sales Capability	☐	☐
Traveling	☐	☐
OTHER	☐	☐

Weaknesses in sales can be boiled down to three areas: mindset, toolset, and skillset. This book will help you build awareness of the mindsets, toolsets and skillsets of elite sales professionals. When addressing weaknesses, see them as opportunities to improve. Focus on one key weakness at a time. Choose the one "big rock" that, if it was removed or minimized, would have the greatest impact on your sales performance. Use the criteria of "current impact," "future impact," and "time frame" (due date/urgency) to set priority for time management.

Assign each separate improvement with "H" for high, "M" for medium, or "L" for Low. Rank improvements vertically for current impact. Then do the same for future impact, then time frame based on urgency. To determine the first weakness to address, look at each improvement line horizontally, and pick the one with the highest ranking. Improvement number one is the winner in the example below:

	CURRENT	FUTURE	TIME FRAME	ACTION STEP
Improvement 1	H	H	H (next week)	Goal Measure
Improvement 2	H	M	L (two months)	Goal Measure
Improvement 3	L	L	M (one month)	Goal Measure

Performance Springboard

Ask yourself, "How can I use my strengths (Gallup or other behavioral-style tools) to overcome my weaknesses? Am I playing to win by taking chances and pushing myself? Am I playing not to lose by playing it safe and accepting excuses for low to mediocre performance results? Am I playing to cruise by not taking action or being ruled by fear?"

Losers visualize the penalties of failure. Winners visualize the rewards of success.

—Unknown

Territory &
Prospect
Management

Territory and Prospect Management

Gone are the days of mindless prospecting, spray and pray marketing, and antiquated list buying. Buyers have evolved, and so must sellers.

There is a growing disconnect between seller prospecting and buyer reaction.

Sellers are frustrated for the following reasons:

- Traditional methods are not working.

- E-mails are not being opened.

- Cold-call appointments are not being accepted.

- Voicemail messages are not being returned.

- Marketing events are not being attended.

- Advertising is not drawing an audience.

- More time is required to attract a diminishing number of prospects.

- Analysis, communication, technology, and social media skills required for efficiency and effectiveness are lacking.

- Roles and responsibilities among sales, marketing, and sales enablement are shifting.

- Fifty percent of sales time is wasted on unproductive prospecting (the B2B Lead).

Unfortunately, there is no app supplying leads that convert quickly. However, using customer relationship management (CRM) tools will improve your communication and activities with leads, prospects, and existing clients. There are new CRMs on the market that do have apps and are cloud-based. New CRMs are using smart technology and providing a personal assistant and customization options. These apps–like Cloze–are creating a better experience for sales representatives and creating many automated functions, so that you can forget about forgetting and be reminded about what is going on with your relationships. Apps that combine and connect–such as Evernote, an app that allows you to capture business card info, and syncs with smart CRMs to update contacts–help you manage relationships so you can close more deals more effectively and efficiently. These cloud-based apps connect easily with other apps, creating the ability to say goodbye to lots of data entry. This is key to having a CRM that works for you versus against you from a time management and benefit perspective. If data entry is a "time sink," it is time for a new, evolved CRM.

The Growing Disconnect Between Seller Prospecting and Buyer Reaction

Buyers are frustrated for the following reasons:

- Communication lacks personalization, value, purpose, and clarity.

- Messaging focuses on vendor products and services–not on resolving customer problems.

- They don't have time to attend nonproductive meetings or events.

- They expect information to be available when they want to buy–not when sellers want to sell.

Eighty-five percent of customers and prospects are unsatisfied with their on-the-phone experience (Salesforce).

Keys to Effective Prospecting

- Make prospecting a priority–prospect every day.

- Focus on a target market or territory–do not over segment.

- Develop buyer personas.

- Actively work a targeted call list.

- Use the preferred communication method of each prospect.

- Master skills in e-mailing, calling, and following up.

- Build a social media presence.

- Develop and send content based on business value and trigger events.

- Inform, educate, and engage prospects with thought leadership.

- Use visuals and video to heighten attention and interest.

- Earn trust by being authentic and doing your homework.

- Ask existing clients for referrals.

    - Ninety-one percent of customers say they would give referrals, but only 11 percent of salespeople ask for them (Dale Carnegie).

- Learn how to use new prospecting tools.

    - Eighty-two percent of prospects can be reached on social media (Sergey Gusarov).

- Fortune is found in the follow-up.

Social Selling

Sales Professional who use social selling are 51 percent more likely to exceed their quota.

—Mike Derezin (VP, Sales, LinkedIn)

Four Pillars of Social Selling

1. Create a professional brand: establish a professional presence on LinkedIn with a complete profile. Consider your audience. Facebook, Twitter, Pinterest, YouTube, Instagram... what else?

2. Find the right people: prospect efficiently with powerful search and research capabilities.

3. Engage with insights: discover and share valuable information to initiate or maintain a relationship and build followers, and join target market groups.

4. Build strong relationships: expand your network to reach prospects and those who can introduce you to prospects.

 ## Performance Springboard

Measure and monitor your prospecting efforts to find out what is working and what is not working. You may also need to try methods that did not work in the past because of lower levels of skill. Find two to three that work for you, and stick to them.

- How is prospecting measured in your organization? Do you have a defined sales process balanced with leading and lagging indicators of success?

- How many qualified opportunities leading to meaningful interactions are needed to attain your revenue goals and meet quota?

- What social media capabilities have you acquired over the past twelve months to increase your prospecting and sales effectiveness?

The Extra Mile

The last three or four reps is what makes the muscle grow. This area of pain divides the champion from someone else who is not a champion.

—Arnold Schwarzenegger

Here's how top-performing salespeople go the extra mile:

- Calling key customers regularly to see if they have issues with which they can help

- Following up quickly when customers call

- Showing appreciation by sending thank-you notes

- Making customer service requests their highest priority

- Providing clients with relevant thought leadership

- Asking customers how they can improve service and providing value in every interaction

Here's how top-performing sales organizations go the extra mile:

- Hiring people who have demonstrated going the extra mile with their customers, communities, colleagues, and families

- Teaching and coaching employees to treat each customer as special, important, and valued

- Encouraging employees to exceed customer expectations

- Empowering employees to solve problems

- Rewarding great service

Performance Springboard

Find small challenges each week. Make five more calls than last week. Reach out to past customers. Look for new markets to try and break into. These are ways to go the extra mile vs. continuing to do the same:

— How do you go the extra mile in support of your customers?

— What do exemplary sales professionals in your organization do to go the extra mile?

— How supportive is your organization in creating a "go the extra mile" culture?

— Given the "ebb and flow" of selling, when are the best times for you to go the extra mile? Is it a time of year or season when you can put in the extra work and elevate your business?

— What are you doing to create more physical and positive energy?

— Do you know what time of day or night you are most effective and productive?

Be Proactive

Be Proactive and Overcommunicate

When in doubt, call the client on the phone or go by their office. This works in all situations. Touching based to add value, confirm, or explain builds trust. Being proactive lets people know you care.

Controlling the Controllable

To minimize the probability and seriousness of "controllable" going sideways, ask these questions:

- What could go wrong? (Potential problem)

- What could cause the potential problem to occur? (Likely cause)

- What action(s) can be taken to eliminate the likely cause and reduce the probability of the likely cause actually causing the potential problem to occur? (Take preventive action)

- What action(s) can I take to reduce the seriousness, should the potential problem occur? (Contingency plan action)

Controlling the Controllable: Sample Scenarios

- Potential problem: A competitor wins the sale.

- Likely cause: A key stakeholder has a relationship with the other vendor.

- Preventive action: Conduct a one-on-one meeting to discuss stakeholder objectives, address questions and concerns, and begin building a relationship.

- Contingency plan action: Propose partnering with the other vendor and utilizing the strengths of each.

Performance Springboard

During the sales process, what are the things you control? Influence? Plan for?

What preventive and contingent actions have you put in place to ensure success?

Be Professional

Without professionalism you are a chump, and the clients I have don't hire chumps. Be a champ by being professional internally and externally.

Sales Professionalism Means Always Doing the Following:

- Exhibiting honesty and integrity

    - Never compromising one's values
    - Always telling the truth
    - Doing the right thing—particularly during demanding situations
    - Keeping one's word to customers and colleagues
    - Maintaining confidentiality

- Taking accountability and responsibility for one's actions

    - Owning the thoughts, actions and words of one's company, one's colleagues, and oneself
    - Following through on requests from customers and colleagues and keeping them informed along the way

- Developing competency

    - Continuously updating industry and customer knowledge
    - Staying ahead of the curve to provide thought leadership to customers and colleagues
    - Continuously developing requisite skills for facilitating the buying/selling process
    - Maximizing the use of data and technology to work more efficiently and effectively
    - Viewing challenges as growth opportunities

- Projecting a positive image

    - Exuding confidence and pride in helping others be successful

    - Projecting a positive attitude

    - Listening more and talking less

    - Mirroring customer values, rules, practices, rituals, and norms

    - Being prepared, organized, focused, and attentive during all interactions with customers and colleagues

- Knowing self and others

- Having the mentality of a champ

- Bringing positive energy

- Demonstrating exemplary time management

- Rigorously preparing each day

- Being proactive

- Going the extra mile

- Control yourself even in high stress situations

- Committing and persevering.

Performance Springboard

On a scale of one to ten, how professional are you when dealing with internal customers? Colleagues?

On a scale of one to ten, how professional are you when dealing with external customers? Suppliers?

What can you do to increase your professionalism for each?

Commitment &
Perseverance

Commitment and Perseverance

The sky is the limit when you commit and persevere. The scariest competition is the one that doesn't quit.

–Evan Sanchez

In all suffering it is important to remember your strengths and your experiences, so you can stay committed to your goals and persevere. If you do this, you will find success and fulfillment even if things don't go exactly as planned.

Here is my personal example:

As a kid growing up in Albuquerque, New Mexico, I played many sports, including soccer, football, wrestling, martial arts, swimming, and water polo. I tried just about anything my parents allowed. My favorites were soccer and football. Football was my favorite of all, but after suffering a broken tibia, I was never able to play again.

My ability to play football was taken away, and I had to pivot to my next-highest sports interest. So soccer became my main sport and my passion. My vision was to be a professional soccer player from that point forward. I suffered many more injuries over the years that called for more knee surgeries–all due to my previous injury suffered playing football. The location of the break in my leg permanently damaged the growth plate. At age thirteen, I had to have both of my tibia growth plates fused to stop the deformity from getting worse in one leg and keep from having one leg longer than the other. I suffered many torn ligaments and much destroyed cartilage due to the deformity, and surgery became a part of my life in sports. I did not feel the pain except when it was so bad I could not run at full speed and had to commit to another surgery. Six weeks later, I was back on the field.

Injuries and pain were not enough to keep me from my passion for soccer and my dreams of playing professionally. I learned to adapt. I learned to play on through pain and discomfort, develop new ball skills and the physical and mental strength to compensate for my new weakness–loss of speed. I learned to ignore the pain and stay focused on my goals for my future. In my final season of high school soccer, I ended the season as one of the top five goal scorers in the state of New Mexico, played for the Olympic development program, and played semiprofessional soccer for the Albuquerque Gunners. I was on track to becoming a professional soccer player and achieving my dreams. All I had to do was stay on track, and I would achieve my vision of success. I believed in myself and had total confidence I would achieve my dream of playing professional soccer.

Following my senior season, I was invited to play in a Thanksgiving tournament. In that tournament, I injured my knee again. After repeated attempts to come back as I had done so many times before, I was done. There was nothing left to repair and I needed a knee replacement at age eighteen. College soccer and the dream of playing as a professional in Europe was no longer a reality for me. My vision of success was shattered. I let negative thinking invade my head, and my championship mentality was not what it had been at my best. Mentally, no setback or obstacle was going to keep me from what I most desired. Physically, I could not have what I most desired. I wanted to be a professional doing what I loved, but my ability to do so was gone.

What was I to do? I did not have another interest to turn to–nowhere to pivot.

It was hard. There were many years that were tough, and at times I would say I just didn't give a shit, so I operated with disregard and little fear, just looking for the next thrill. My limiting beliefs were that

I was a has-been. I was supposed to be a professional athlete. All I had ever dreamed of was not to be. I wasn't special anymore.

In order to live a normal active lifestyle, I had to work out and develop my leg muscles to support the loss of my irreparable ligaments and cartilage. I needed a replacement, but I was so young the doctors told me to wait in the hopes the technology increases would allow better solution for the future repair versus getting a knee replacement every ten years. So I worked out and trained with body builders who helped me to improve my strength and balance in my leg. This led me to start my own business as a personal trainer–the beginning of my next pivot. I developed intuitive flow and found my entrepreneur spirit. I pivoted and transformed into a corporate athlete. This was something I had never envisioned doing, but I am grateful for finding a new passion where it is not all about me. If I had just given up, I would not be who I am today.

My success in sports had instilled a championship mentality. I have the confidence and the "no quit" attitude combined with the knowledge and experience of success. I was a professional when it came to championship mindsets. I was successful at overcoming adversity and finding new ways to win. Perseverance and commitment allowed me to find success in new areas of life.

I have been up, down, and all turned around at times. But when I find my center and look back at my successes and failures, I can always find a way to climb back to the top. Commitment and perseverance will bring you the success and resilience needed in life and in sales.

Performance Springboard

Top sales people make a habit of generating opportunities in these ways:

- Seeking out challenges

- Exhibiting self-confidence

- Building on their strengths

- Taking calculated risks

- Seeing the glass as half full

- Being curious as to what's going on around them

- Making bold choices

- Buildings on what's working

- Doing what they say they will do for their clients and prospects

Sales Champions Keep these Things in Mind:

- Mental toughness is required to stay committed and perse-vere, and positive thinking is better than negative thinking in the long run.

- Positive thinking needs to be grounded in critical thinking in order to rationally define next steps and set priority on tasks necessary for improvement, as opposed to telling yourself you are better than you really are. This type of positivity hinders performance when not balanced with critical thinking.

- Champions develop mental toughness, and this mental tough-ness can keep you going in the face of any adversity.

— Complex sales can take a long time. Budgets, strategic priority changes, reorganizations, and many other business-related challenges can keep your buyers from buying when they want to do so. Commitment to these buyers will bring success in the future.

— Perseverance will lead you to winning buyers who may have said "no" to you in the past. In sales, your fortune can be made in persistent and professional follow up.

Mental toughness means taking control of your thoughts, feelings, and attitudes... especially under pressure.

–Steve Siebold

177 Mental Toughness Secrets of the World Class is the best book and system to build mental toughness and thinking strategies that will help you persevere when faced with adversity.

Sell Like
A Champ

Sell Like a Champ

There is no viable way to sell like a champ without having a sales process. Prior to having formal sales process and skills training, I believed I had good days and bad days when it came to sales. When you create a sales process that is focused on the buyer, it allows you to focus on helping the buyer find what they need in a way that feels conversational. Combining a customer focused sales process with behavioral preferences and sales skills will improve your ability to build trust and rapport quickly. You will create a better connection with the buyer, and you will significantly improve your close ratios and average sales cycle time.

Typical sales skills include the following:

- Prospecting/social selling

- Qualifying buyers

- Elevator speeches, capability statements, or value propositions

- Open- and closed-ended questions

- Situations, problems, and needs discoveries

- Soft closes and go negatives

- Transitions to closing statements

- Closing

- Managing the account

- Dealing with objections

These skills are necessary to any sales process. In order to sell like a champ, you will need to master them all while meeting the individual or collective emotional drivers of your prospects.

You will need advanced selling skills.

Advanced selling skills include the following:

- Knowing your style, the way you walk and talk, and the impression you make on others

- Controlling yourself by being tolerant and considerate of others' preferences without becoming irritated

- Knowing the prospect's style and seeing the dialectic tension raised based on your messages and questions. Know when to raise or lower tension to improve the sales experience and get them to buy faster. The sales experience is emotionally based, and being able to improve the mood will improve your close ratios.

- Doing something for others to make them comfortable. If you talk faster than they do, slow down. If you talk slower, speed up. This will go a long way in building trust and the positive emotions that make them want to buy from you now and in the future.

- Understanding the unique style needs at each stage of the selling process.

This is where the use of social styles in your selling process really pays off. If you are selling the way you would like to be sold to, you will be successful about 25 percent of the time if you close every deal you submit for signature. To sell like a champ, you will need to sell to the buyer in a way they would like to be sold to–this is why our number one behavior and skill set is "know yourself" and improve your EQ. Learning your style and modifying your behavior to build rapport is the number one way to turn a chump or a contender into a sales champ.

In the pages that follow, you will learn the key modifications to make per the buyer to improve your close ratios and sales cycle times.

Sales Champs know where they are in the sales process and the emotional buy-in of the prospect within each conversation. Knowing where you are in the process is very important to moving the sale forward with each objective you achieve. If the prospect is at "no interest," you want to create interest and get a meaningful interaction going. Once you have the meeting, you want to ask questions to understand potential ways to help the buyer by understanding their situations and problems. This is "low interest." "High interest" involves a deeper understanding of the issue or needs of the buyer. Is it worth resolving? How does this hurt them or make them look bad? What do the solutions look like? How will removing the pain make them feel? What kind of positive effects will come from the right kind of solution? If you can understand these key points, you can transition the conversation into a solution and ask to present a proposal. Getting them to say "yes" here moves them to "converted." Getting the proposal signed moves the buyer to "invest"–and means a payday for you for closing the business. You don't want to be offering solutions to their business if you haven't even been able to create a meaningful conversation. That is called "show up and throw up." That's for chumps. You can't be closing a large-scale deal if you haven't positioned the value. That's for chumps. Know where you are in the process, and modify your selling skills for each stage to sell like a champ.

Where are *You* and the Prospect in the Sales Process?

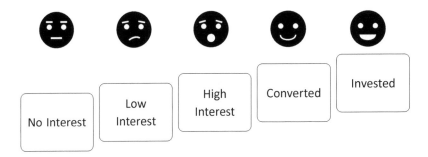

In a more transactional sales environment, there is still a process. There may not even be a need for salespeople, but a process is still important. For example, take a new software app that lets you try before you buy. You enter your user info, and if you like the app or service, the company simply charges your card after the trial period is over. No relationship needed or complexity to explain. This is still a sales process that is in line with the customer expectation but has no connection to a sales professional.

As you move up the ladder of complexity, more research and comparison of alternatives is necessary. Buyers are now searching the Internet and comparing products and services themselves prior to speaking to sales professionals. In some cases, online sales agents will pop up to offer help, and now artificial intelligence bots are being implemented for low complexity sales. Some are blending messenger bots and people for a combination of AI and human interaction. In order to do this, there must be a strong process and customer journey map in place to provide a good experience for the buyer. A terrible experience would feel like when you get lost in the black hole of phone-tree hell. When that happens, you lose the prospect. These changes in technology only make it more important to know where your buyer is in the sales process and act accordingly to improve the experience and close more deals.

The key to success for any human is EQ, and AI cannot replace EQ–for now, anyway. Research shows that the higher the level of complexity, the more the sales professional's selling style is key to producing results. Even more research shows that the challenger style is the most successful with high levels of complexity. I don't care what type of style you use–they can all be improved by knowing where you are in the sales process and getting an emotional buy-in correlated to the prospect's behavior style.

In 2009, the Corporate Executive Board (CEB) set out to answer this fundamental question: "What skills, behaviors, knowledge, and attributes matter most for high-performance sales teams?" Specifically, the CEB

- initially surveyed hundreds of front-line sales managers spanning nearly one hundred countries, and has surveyed more than 6,000 sales reps globally since the initial survey;

- instructed each sales manager to assess three sales reps they directly managed–on average, two sales reps and one star or high performer across forty-four different attributes;

- included every major industry, geography, and go-to-market model in the survey;

- asked sales managers to assess each sales rep's attitude, the degree to which the sales rep worked to solve customer issues, and the sales rep's willingness to risk disapproval;

- analyzed the skills, behaviors, activities, and knowledge of the customer's business and of the sales rep's own company's solutions;

- addressed the sales rep's tenure, geography, account size, direct versus indirect, and general territory versus named account; and

- utilized "performance against quota" as the prevailing metric to gauge overall effectiveness.

The sales styles broke down to the following groupings:

- Hard worker: Willing to do what it takes. May need to work smarter.

- Problem solver: Focuses on issues, generally not a people person.

- Relationship focused: Limited focus on business issues with strong people skills.

- Lone wolf: Intuitive style and not replicable.

- Challenger: the challenger is distinguished by the ability to teach, take control of the process, and tailor the solution.

As the levels of complexity in the sale increases, the challenger raises to the top in percentage of sales champs. The challenger outperforms all styles in more complicated sales. The closest is the lone wolf, but this style is not one you can model as a method to build a team. Leveraging *Sell like a Champ* is your best way to build a team of "A" players and dominate your competition.

Sell Like
A Champ

All styles can improve performance by improving EQ!

Where are *You* and the Prospect in the Sales Process?

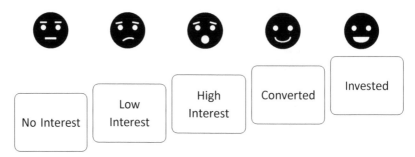

To be a sales champ, you need to know the desirable traits for each behavior style. The approach and value proposition you use may be the most important step in connecting with your prospect. That first interaction should pique interest in you and your product or service and move the buyer from "no interest" to "low interest." Take time to understand their style, and formulate an approach to fit. Sales is an emotional process, and you need to appeal to those that are controlled or highly emotional to connect with trust. Do they talk slow or fast? Do they talk loud of soft? Slow and soft will tell you they are most likely an "analytical" or "amiable." Talking fast and loud will tell you they are most likely an "expressive" or" driver." Relationship topics point to amiable and expressive while project timelines and goals point more toward analytical and driving social styles.

Analyticals share the overall goal and need to be right. In early sales stages, you and your value proposition should

- show accuracy,

- save them face in front of their peers,

- be on time,

- be formal, and

- get to business quickly.

Drivers share the overall goal and need to be in control. In early sales stages, you and your value proposition should

- save them time,

- be on time,

- be fast-paced, and

- provide options.

Amiables share the overall goal and need to have stability and harmony with others. In early sales stages you and your value proposition should

- protect them from conflict,

- be relaxed,

- come to mutual agreement, and

- invite conversation.

Expressives share the overall goal and need to be recognized as significant. In early sales stages you and your value proposition should

- save them effort,

- be energetic and fast-paced,

- use testimonials, and

- create a competitive spirit.

When interviewing, the lists below will help you appeal to each style.

Task focused–Analytical:

- Appeal to their logical side.

- Be detailed.

- Be businesslike.

- Avoid too much social or small talk.

Driver:

- Be prepared and fast-paced.

- Be professional and confident.

- Be results-oriented.

- Show you have done your homework.

Relationship focused–Amiable:

- Be casual and easygoing.

- Project warmth.

- Demonstrate interest in them as a person.

- Focus on building trust and credibility.

Expressive:

- Let them set the pace and direction of the meeting.

- Be animated and enthusiastic.

- Give them recognition and admiration.

- Be creative and supportive of their ideas.

In demonstrating value, the lists below will help you appeal to each style.

Task focused–Analytical:

- Emphasize accuracy.

- Show value and ROI.

- Demonstrate quality and reliability.

- Include pros and cons.

Driver:

- Emphasize efficiency.

- Show potential gains and profits.

- Show savings.

Relationship focused–Amiable:

- Emphasize security.

- Demonstrate steadiness.

- Minimize risk.

Expressive:

- Emphasize excitement.

- Show uniqueness.

— Decrease effort for them.

Reduce concerns like a sales champ. Do this based on the prospect's style to reduce objections, build trust, and accelerate cycle time.

Task focused–Analytical:

— They want facts.

— They want you to anticipate their objections and potential risks.

— They want you to make commitments you can keep.

— They don't want to be pushed or hurried.

— They want you to show them how this is an investment and not an expenditure.

— They want proof.

Driver:

— They want to know clearly and specifically what's going to happen and by when.

— They want quick answers and results-oriented benefits.

— They want you to be brief and to the point.

— They want to know the results they can expect.

— They want to know the bottom line.

— They want specific bullets outlining end results.

— They want to know how your product or service is going to profit them.

Relationship focused–Amiable:

- They want answers to their many questions.

- They want patient explanations.

- They want zero selling pressure.

- They don't want to be the first to try a product.

- They want proof and minimal risk.

- They want you to be personable.

- They want to understand the features of your product or service

Expressive:

- They want proof of how your product or service will provide them enjoyment.

- They want you to tell them how it will make others happy.

- They want to know how it will bring them recognition or appreciation.

- They need to know that you'll be around to follow up and support them when problems arise.

Manage any account like a sales champ with these guides.

Task focused–Analytical

- Follow a timetable for measuring results.

- Deliver on promises.

Driver:

- Provide reminders of your track record.

- Respond with quick solutions to problems.

Relationship focused–Amiable

- Practice consistent and predictable service.

- Provide personal attention.

Expressive

- Check in regularly to ensure tasks are aligned.

- Save them complications and paperwork.

 Performance Springboard

Sales champs need a business model that helps to motivate the buyer.

There are some business models that are better than others for creating a customer experience that facilitates buyers taking action. How many times have you heard members of your sales team say, "The buyer just isn't ready to buy?" How many times have you heard the famous "Call me back next month" buyer push for not making a decision? If you hear this often, it may not be the salesperson's responsibility to improve. It may also be time to look at the sales culture and business model to build in four key motivating impulses that get prospects to take action.

The Four Motivating Impulses:

1. Fear of Loss: People are motivated and more likely to take action if something is a hot item and there is a limited quantity available. This situation creates an impulse in any human to take action if something of value could be lost–especially to the competition.

2. Urgency: Similar to the fear of loss but slightly different, the sense of urgency creates action because the buyer is compelled to act quickly. If the buyer gets it first, they are making sure they don't miss out, and they get to be the trend setter. Have you ever noticed that people selling a hot item are quick to qualify, and if you are not ready to buy, they are quick to move on? This sense of urgency in the business and salesperson creates urgency in the buyer as well.

3. The Jones Effect: There was a movie made about this one titled *Keeping up with the Joneses*, though the title has now been stolen by the Kardashians–*Keeping up with the Kardashians*. Keeping up with the Joneses is when the buyer is buying something that others have in order to keep up or meet a perceived benchmark. This could be tapping into vanity, greed, or jealousy, but this is a true human impulse that appears in the business world by way of keeping up with your competition. If the competition is using some new tool or marketing scheme that may also help you, you want it. The Jones effect is very powerful, and it is why celebrities get paid so much money to endorse products. It is also why word of mouth continues to be the best form of marketing. We want what others around us have.

4. Consultative: This is really the basis for good and honest consultative sales. The salesperson listens to the buyer's needs and lets them know if they can help or not. If they can, they

will provide two or three value-based options based on the issues that need to be resolved. The buyer gets to make the decision moving forward without unnecessary pressure to buy. This is a consultative approach. However, if my business model helped to create the fear of loss, urgency, and the Jones effect, being consultative would be very easy. The salesperson would offer two to three options and lets the buyer decide which one they would like to move forward with while internally, the buyer's emotions have persuaded them to make a decision to buy.

Any business that can build all four into their customer experience will make it easier for their sales team to sell like a champ. The more impulses combined, the higher the likelihood of the buyer taking action.

Here is an example of this model at work.

I was a sales executive for a local business journal publication that did weekly top twenty-five lists. This business model really tapped into all of the impulses mentioned above in the following ways.

I knew the editorial calendar and the top list winners from each previous year. I knew who the qualified buyers were, and I could also call on industries that wanted to be in front of the companies on the upcoming list. So I knew who to call and had qualified buyers because of the business model. Qualified buyers combined with urgency improves sales cycle times and close ratios. I could call each industry list and get them to enter to be part of the list and see if they wanted to buy an ad because of the business model. This was a value to the buyer and a nonpushy benefit call to the prospect to create urgency.

So, who do you think I called first? In order to leverage all the impulses set up by the business model, I called number one on the list from the previous year. I would offer them the best location first and let them know that I would be calling the others on the list the next day, so I needed to know if they were interested in premium add placement. This one phone call enacted the fear of loss, sense of urgency, the Jones effect, and the consultative approach and created a situation for the buyer to take action. This worked for all the calls that followed as well—not just for the number one position but for each prospect. I continued to call as I made my way down the list. The space was limited, I was calling the whole list, I was giving them one day to respond, and I would take the first to call. Motivation to take action was set.

Is your business model set up to create this type of positive environment for your sales team? What changes to your business model could be made to improve the selling environment to get buyers excited to do business with you today?

Put Your Vision into Action!

We have covered the mindsets, toolsets, and skillsets for peak performance in sales. Now it is up to you to make it happen.

- What mindsets do you need to apply to elevate your thinking so you can elevate your performance?

- Where are you not satisfied in your personal or professional performance?

- What behaviors, skillsets, and toolsets do you need to implement and practice to elevate your performance?

- Where do you want to be in three years?

- Where do you want to be in one year?

- Where do you want to be in six months?

- Where do you want to be in three months?

Go Sell Like a Champ!

For more resources and support visit

www.SellLikeAChamp.com

Made in the USA
Columbia, SC
09 December 2017